06

06/30

Prayer of the Child Mystic

Prayer of the Child Mystic

Published by

Contemplative Publications
P.O. Box 5435
Manchester, New Hampshire   03108-5435

ISBN-13:   978-0-9777612-0-3
ISBN-10:   0-9777612-0-7

Library of Congress Control Number: 2006901001

Printed in the United States of America

Prayer of the
Child Mystic

Ken Lazdowski

Photographs by Gail Lee

"Except ye be converted, and become as little children,
ye shall not enter into the kingdom of heaven."
Matthew 18:3

Invitation

This little book is not for children of all ages; it is for all children without age. These simple prayers are the contemplation of one who is not burdened by the concepts of time and space. Here is a childlike consciousness with no regrets about the past and no worries about the future. What was matters not; what will be matters not. *Is* matters: Who and What really *is*.

The child mystic is not concerned with attaining the admirable qualities of manhood or womanhood but is awakening to the state of Christhood. He is a humble child of God who is on the path of soul discovery. She is an innocent child of God with a growing awareness of spiritual reality.

In each of us there is a child mystic who enjoys a relationship of eternal oneness with all that God is. Yet ignorance of spiritual principle and forgetfulness of our divine heritage have most of us on an endless search for the way back to a kingdom we never left. However, at any moment of the day we may accept the open invitation of the Christ to "know Thee the only true God," and in that knowledge we immediately find ourselves at home, safe and secure, complete and content in the presence of infinite Love. We do this by remembering the nature of reality and meditating on the simple truth of God. For that purpose and that practice, we may begin by contemplating a child's verse as the basis of spiritual maturity and freedom. Every time we recall and relive a prayer of the child mystic, we accept the invitation to "worship the Father in spirit and in truth."

*"Meditate upon these things; give thyself wholly to them;
that thy profiting may appear to all."*
1 Timothy 4:15

Prayer of the Child Mystic

God is good, and God is one.

God is Earth, and God is Sun.

God is Peace, and God is Joy.

God is Girl, and God is Boy.

God is Life, and God is Love.

God is below, and God is above.

God is here, and God is now.

God is why, and God is how.

God is Spirit, and God is Soul.

God is perfect, and God is whole.

God is All, and God is true.

God is Me, and God is You.

"The Lord is good to all:
and His tender mercies are over all His works."
Psalm 145:9

God Is Good

God is the good in all that is real.
It is something we know and something we feel.
Each wonder of God, whether big or small,
Has to be good, having no choice at all.

No matter what we hear or what we see,
The goodness of God will always be,
Not just for little angels who do no wrong,
Not just for saints who pray all day long.

In every child of our Parent divine
The seed of goodness flowers in time,
Not because we believe that it should,
But simply because God is good.

"There is one God; and there is none other."
Mark 12:32

God Is One

There is only one God and not any more.
There cannot be two or three or four.
God is so big, and God is so vast,
The One who is first also is last.

Since God is one, and there is no other,
God is both our Father and Mother.
No presence, no power, no principle but One,
No enemy or force against daughter or son.

Every being, every creature, every plant everywhere
Is one with God in the life that we share.
Beside God, outside God, there really is none,
For God, being God, is the infinite One.

" 'Do not I fill heaven and earth?' saith the Lord."
Jeremiah 23:24

God Is Earth

God made all that was made right from the start,
Using only the best so it wouldn't fall apart.
The universe came first in time and space;
Then stars and planets were put in their place.

Earth's oceans and lakes, rivers and streams
Couldn't be lovelier in our loveliest of dreams.
Mountains were crafted and topped with snow,
While it rained in valleys for daisies to grow.

The land where we live, the waves on the seas,
The air we breathe, and a forest of trees:
Thus God fills the world beyond worth.
More than its creator, God is the Earth.

"God is light, and in Him is no darkness at all."
1 John 1:5

God Is Sun

How can it be, this thing in the sky,
Day after day shining on high?
Is it really and truly only a star,
Like any other, just not as far?

Or might it still be Mystery
That keeps us warm and lets us see?
Wherever we go, whatever we do,
Forever it is with me and you.

Not up there, as it would appear,
But deep within to brighten and cheer,
Burns the fire of Spirit that gives all light,
Where God is Sun and there is no night.

*"Peace I leave with you, My peace I give unto you:
not as the world giveth, give I unto you."*
John 14:27

God Is Peace

So long ago it all began,
No one remembers the original plan,
Not for a battle with victory,
But for peace without any history.

Age after age and still we pray
That peace on Earth will be someday.
But until we know what peace is about,
Our conflicts continue inside and out.

We need not struggle with might or mind
Or neighbor or nation once we find
That everyone's peace, everlasting and real,
Is present in all as God's presence to feel.

*"These things have I spoken unto you, that My joy
might remain in you, and that your joy might be full."
John 15:11*

God Is Joy

Something is happening, and it's all around.
Listen not with ears for this cheerful sound.
Someone is singing a silent song
Of heartfelt gladness all day long.

Something is stirring, and it's all a delight.
Look not with eyes for this charming sight.
Someone is playing at life with fun,
Happy to be God's daughter or son.

Something is dawning, and how bright it seems.
Seek not with senses for this that beams.
Someone is smiling: none other than you,
When the Joy that is God comes shining through.

"So God created man in His own image, in the image of God created He him; male and female created He them."
Genesis 1:27

God Is Girl

The child I am, I am of Thee,
Whose very life Thou gavest me.
The love I have, that love is Thine,
Sustaining me always, Mother Divine.

Each woman I honor, I honor in Thee,
The one maternal Deity.
All sisters I cherish, I cherish in heart:
Thy family, my family, never apart.

Every daughter I see, I see as Thee,
In all Thy sacred femininity.
The infant I hold, I hold her near,
Knowing God is Girl, most precious and dear.

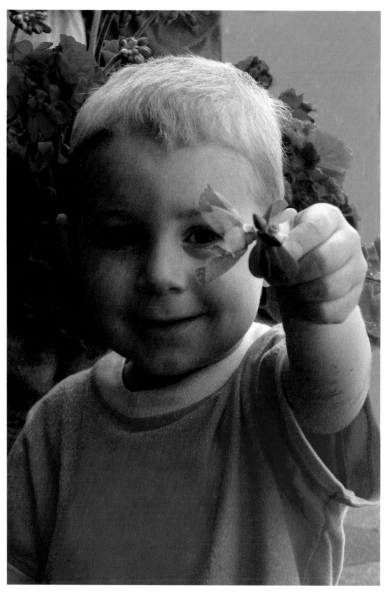

"Beloved, now are we the sons of God."
1 John 3:2

God Is Boy

My Father, my Mother, my Parent blest,
To know Thee aright is my only quest.
My Lord and my God, Thou art in word,
Yet such from Thee, I have not heard.

Thy face is hidden and Thine hands unseen.
Then what of my sonship is there to glean,
Except the constant love I find
With open heart and quiet mind?

This sacred affection assures me throughout
What oneness of being is all about:
Every son of God is the God that is true,
Making God the Boy that I am too.

"He is thy life, and the length of thy days."
Deuteronomy 30:20

God Is Life

This be the day of thanks and praise
For the Lord of life and all His ways,
For every wonder of our very being,
For everyday miracles like hearing and seeing.

We embrace the One as God of the living,
Who of Himself is forever giving
The breath of life to each body and soul,
Keeping His universe alive and whole.

We have no beginning; we have no end.
Birth and death are what we pretend
To be our doorways in a world of strife
That does not exist because God is Life.

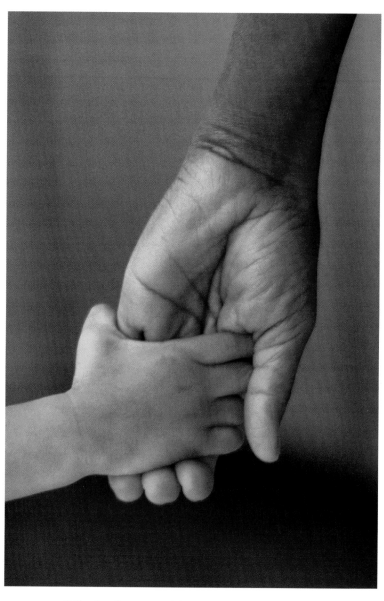

"God is love; and he that dwelleth in love
dwelleth in God, and God in him."
1 John 4:16

God Is Love

Before all time, there was nothing but Love,
Neither ground underfoot, nor sky above.
Not a man or a woman or a child anywhere,
Not even an angel or a heaven was there.

Love loved Itself and loving so much,
Love could not help being as such.
So Love expressed life, and life It is still,
Forming all that is real, as Love always will.

The cause, the purpose, the essence of all,
The law, the power, the wherewithal,
Is purely the love of the Love that is pure,
Who we of Love know is God for sure.

"Know therefore this day, and consider it in thine heart,
that the Lord, He is God in heaven above,
and upon the earth beneath: there is none else."
Deuteronomy 4:39

God Is Below

I awaken in the valley without walls or roof,
Yet never with a longing for shelter as proof
That God is with me because I have found
No matter how low, this is holy ground.

I walk His field in the shadow of hills
With one straw basket the Lord always fills.
Blessed with more treasure He did bequeath,
I fish the stream and His waters beneath.

I rest in the night under stars and moon
With a soul-felt peace not leaving soon.
My prayer is gratitude every depth I go,
For there I learn God too is below.

"For thou, Lord, art high above all the earth."
Psalm 97:9

God Is Above

Another mountain I begin to climb
With ever more faith and hope this time
That I may find the dwelling of God,
The holy summit of Him I laud.

Along the upward path there be
One of wisdom who waits for me
With loving guidance and much to teach
About the way and the goal to reach.

Atop the world, beyond every cloud,
Not a thing to sense but the Silence loud.
"'Tis the God above," the sage does tell.
"We brought Him with us: Immanuel."

*"Then shalt thou call, and the Lord shall answer;
thou shalt cry, and He shall say, 'Here I am.'"
Isaiah 58:9*

God Is Here

No need to lament those churches and shrines
Now vacant and cold where no candle shines
To honor the God we thought we knew,
For never was He the one who withdrew.

No need for a journey to faraway lands
Across oceans, mountains and desert sands
To search for God as many have tried,
Since Omnipresence cannot hide.

No need to pray for the Spirit of grace
To enter our dreams of time and space.
Wake up instead, and the truth will appear:
As the I that I AM, God is here.

"I am with you always."
Matthew 28:20

God Is Now

Once upon an age, according to tradition,

The Lord of ancients ruled in Eden with a mission:

Oneness with man and woman. But union did not last,

Unlike the separation while God is in the past.

Once upon a promise, according to tale and song,

The Lord to come for faithfuls shall do away with wrong.

Thus on and on the wait for Him to end all sorrow,

As long as God is kept devoutly in tomorrow.

Once upon awakening, according to reality,

The Lord of truth is Being this moment in eternity.

Never before or after is the One to whom we bow.

I AM solely in the present, for the only God is now.

"Whatsoever the Lord pleased, that did He in heaven,
and in earth, in the seas, and all deep places."
Psalm 135:6

God Is Why

I ponder at length this cosmos of treasure,
Its beauty and order in such grand measure.
I wonder at times about blue and green,
And how things can be the way they seem.

I think about thinking and the reason for thought;
Why being, why breathing, why doing, why not;
How to explain a child's learning and growing;
Even the purpose of our coming and going.

I pray for an answer to life's biggest question,
Unwilling to surmise or make a suggestion.
Waiting in silence for the ultimate reply,
Comes the whisper of Soul that God is why.

"With God all things are possible."
Mark 10:27

God Is How

Personal life evolves as so much to do,
Thoughts overwhelm us of how to get through
Our difficult times that appear not to end
In spite of the effort we constantly spend.

Then there are others who seem to oppose
Our best of intentions in the manner of foes.
Such people and things surely must yield,
But how for us without power to wield?

Every limit is within and nothing outer;
Every challenge is self, the ultimate doubter.
The bridge to true freedom is crossed on the day
We learn God is the how because I AM the way.

"God is spirit: and they that worship Him
must worship Him in spirit and in truth."
John 4:24

God Is Spirit

O Lord our God, we know You are, but not what You are.

I AM like the wind on the sea that sails your ship afar.

I AM like the air you breathe without a thought for breath.

I AM like the warmth in heart when love possesses depth.

O dear Lord, we hear of You, but do not understand.

I AM like inspiration moving the artist's hand.

I AM like idea behind manifestation.

I AM like awareness in silent meditation.

O dear God, we see Your likeness, but You, we do not.

The vision is yours, My children, unless you forgot.

You behold what I AM as you draw ever near it.

Divine mystery unveiled, the answer is Spirit.

"I will put My spirit within you."
Ezekiel 36:27

God Is Soul

Given the lessons we faithfully read
And all our study, there is still the need
To transcend our books, no matter how sound,
For not on a page is God to be found.

Holy men and women we deeply respect
As teachers of truth on which we reflect
To lift our state beyond humankind,
Where even the saintly are left behind.

All of the scriptures and sages as well
Point to the inside of our mortal shell.
The "pearl of great price" is no outer role,
But God within, being the I of Soul.

"As for God, His way is perfect."
2 Samuel 22:31

God Is Perfect

If only I were older and all grown up,
I would change the world by sharing a cup
Of love and peace with all for the better,
As a giver of joy and not just a getter.

If only I were younger and in my prime,
I would change the world by spending more time
With people of need, to improve their lot,
As a servant in deed and not just in thought.

If only I were God and knew perfectly well
How perfect His world in which we dwell,
I would change my view, for without exception,
Whatever of God, it is perfection.

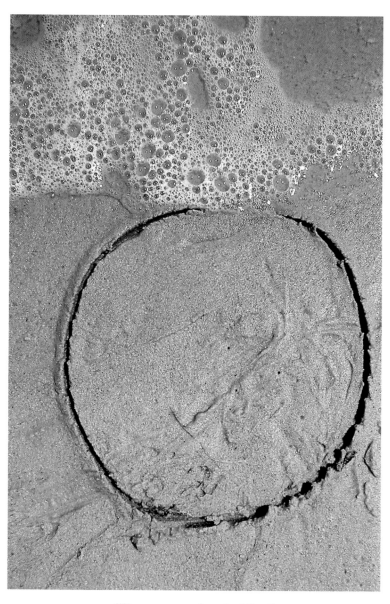

"Ye are complete in Him."
Colossians 2:10

God Is Whole

In the beginning by grace was the miracle done,
Eternally perfect, complete, and one.
In the image and likeness of God we were made
With His soundness and glory that never fade.

Every blessing we pray for us to be shown,
In essence and form, is already our own.
No matter the claim, our position is wealth.
No matter its name, our condition is health.

The truth of being to us revealed
Is the simple secret of our being healed.
God living as us is the One we extol,
Wholly spiritual and spiritually whole.

"Christ is all, and in all."
Colossians 3:11

God Is All

God is All but nothing we believe.

God is All but nothing we conceive.

God is All but nothing we perceive.

God is All but nothing we achieve.

God is Each of us but no one born.

God is Everyone but none we mourn.

God is Everything having no opposite.

God is All and more than the sum of it.

God is All behind the scene.

God is All beyond the dream.

God is All without condition.

God is All past definition.

*"Enter into His gates with thanksgiving, and into His courts
with praise: be thankful unto Him, and bless His name.
For the Lord is good; His mercy is everlasting;
and His truth endureth to all generations."
Psalm 100:4,5*

God Is True

Should we hear any rumors of storm or war,
Let us not bid them enter, but close the door
Of the temple within to every false power,
And ascend with the True into Its high tower.

Should we face an appearance of lack or ill,
Let us not be deceived, but trust divine will
Only to be for the bliss we have sought.
All else is unreal and thus ever naught.

Should we be tempted of person or of place,
Let us not pursue idols, but end the chase
After shadows empty through and through,
To rest with faith in the One who is true.

"I am the way, the truth, and the life:
no man cometh unto the Father, but by Me."
John 14:6

God Is Me

Giving up my ways, I turn within,
Forgiven all and free to begin
Looking, listening, and living for Love,
Content to be a servant thereof.

Praying that ego is left behind,
This path continues beyond the mind
Toward a sense of being not my own,
A sacred realm completely unknown.

Lost in love for the mystical Lord,
Soul is lifted where never man soared:
Into the light of Divinity.
Then self is no more, and God is Me.

"I have said, 'Ye are gods;
and all of you are children of the most High.'"
Psalm 82:6

God Is You

Since the joy of the Lord exceeds all measure,
The infinite universe is His pleasure
To experience through You this very day
In love, in work, and even in play.

Spirit so much wants to sing and dance
As the soul You are at every chance.
God's will to create must be fulfilled
Right here and now in the good You build.

Arise, and serve in motion and rest
His purpose divine of living blessed.
All that God wishes ever to do
Can only be done by being You.

"I and My Father are one."
John 10:30

Prayer of the Child Christ

I AM good, and I AM one.

I AM Earth, and I AM Sun.

I AM Peace, and I AM Joy.

I AM Girl, and I AM Boy.

I AM Life, and I AM Love.

I AM below, and I AM above.

I AM here, and I AM now.

I AM why, and I AM how.

I AM Spirit, and I AM Soul.

I AM perfect, and I AM whole.

I AM All, and I AM true.

I AM Me, and I AM You.

Ken Lazdowski is a practitioner and lecturer of spiritual principles revealed in the teachings of Jesus and the mysticism of Joel S. Goldsmith. He shares this spiritual way of life, love, and prayer at classes and retreats throughout the country. Ken also has a technical career at a research and development center. He and his wife live in New Hampshire with their two daughters.

For additional information, please contact:

Ken Lazdowski
P.O. Box 483
Hudson, NH   03051-0483

Phone: (603) 595-6973
Fax: (603) 578-3451
Email: info@KenLazdowski.com

Gail Lee is a painter, photographer, and printmaker with a degree in Fine Arts from the University of Georgia. She has long been a student of spirituality and practical mysticism. Gail lives in New York with her husband and has two daughters and two granddaughters.

Gail may be contacted at the following email address:

glee500@aol.com